Note to Parents

Here is a collection of gift ideas that children will really enjoy—not only because the gifts are fun to make, but because they are attractive and "good enough to give." Suggestions for creative cards and gift wraps are also included.

Preschoolers will need help with the directions and with the parts of projects that require cutting, sewing, or cooking. The Jiminy Cricket symbol appears with any project that may require adult help. Older children will be able to handle most projects on their own.

Most of the gifts use materials that can be found in the home—cardboard tubes, empty bottles, buttons, and fabric scraps. The few items you may need to buy, such as small plants or artificial flowers, are inexpensive and easy to find. Where gluing is called for, you can use any white glue or substitute a glue stick, which most young children can handle easily.

This book can help your child discover the pleasure of making gifts for friends and for grown-ups, too. They'll take pride in saying, "I made it for you."

I Made It for You!

Presents and Cards to Make

Published by
World Book Encyclopedia, Inc.
a Scott Fetzer company
Chicago

Dr. Rattlebox and the Wonder Bundle

Morty and Ferdie had been saving money for a long time to buy their Uncle Mickey a really nice birthday gift. On the day before Mickey's birthday, they took the money out of their banks and counted it.

"I've got $2.48," said Morty, as he gathered up all his coins and stuffed them into his pockets.

"And I've got $2.52," said Ferdie. "We should be able to buy Uncle Mickey two great presents with all of this money."

Morty and Ferdie started downtown, humming and skipping as they went. They hadn't decided what they would buy yet, but they knew it would have to be very special.

When Morty and Ferdie were about halfway downtown, they saw a man standing on the street corner. In front of him was a very large box with many smaller boxes piled on top.

As Morty and Ferdie got closer, the man began to shout, "Get your magic Wonder Bundle here. Be the first one on your block to own one of Dr. Rattlebox's marvelous, magic Wonder Bundles! You can shake it and rattle it. You can open it up and play with it. There are one dozen things in it—no two alike!"

Morty and Ferdie moved in closer to get a better look at the Wonder Bundles. "Good day, young men," Dr. Rattlebox said. "Where are you going this fine day?"

"We're on our way downtown," said Ferdie. "We're going to buy our Uncle Mickey some great birthday gifts."

"I've got $2.48," said Morty. "And Ferdie has $2.52. So we can get really good presents."

Morty and Ferdie looked at the Wonder Bundles. Then Ferdie picked one of them up and shook it. It *did* rattle. In fact, it rattled a lot. He handed the Wonder Bundle to Morty, and Morty shook it.

"I wonder what makes the box rattle," said Morty. "And I wonder if Uncle Mickey would like to have a Wonder Bundle for his birthday. One of us could get him a Wonder Bundle."

"Dr. Rattlebox," Ferdie said, "how much does one of your Wonder Bundles cost?"

Dr. Rattlebox scratched his head. Then he answered, "I'll tell you what I'm going to do. I am going to let you have one of these marvelous, magic Wonder Bundles for only $5.00. And I know you won't find a bigger surprise anywhere for less than that!"

Morty and Ferdie looked at each other. "That's too bad," said Morty. "Neither of us has that much money. I guess we'll have to get something else." Morty and Ferdie looked down and sadly walked away.

When they were about half a block away from Dr. Rattlebox, Morty and Ferdie stopped suddenly. "Hey," said Ferdie. "I've got $2.52, and you've got $2.48. Together, we do have $5.00. We can go together and get a Wonder Bundle for Uncle Mickey!"

"That's great!" said Morty. "Let's go!"

Morty and Ferdie ran back to Dr. Rattlebox and gave him their money. "A wise decision, boys," he said as he gave them the Wonder Bundle. "Now, don't open the box until you get home. It's bad luck!" He packed up his things and quickly went on his way.

"Come on, Morty," said Ferdie. "Let's show Minnie the present. Will she be surprised!"

Before long, Morty and Ferdie were at Minnie's house. "Hi," said Minnie. "What have you got there? Did you get your Uncle Mickey a birthday gift?"

"Oh, yes," said Morty. "It's a marvelous, magic Wonder Bundle. Just wait till you see what's in it."

Morty and Ferdie opened the box. Inside was a piece of cloth—and under the cloth were one dozen pebbles! "Oh, no!" said Ferdie. "This is nothing but an old box, a dozen worthless rocks, and a piece of cloth. And we used all our money for this!"

"One dozen different things!" Morty muttered. "It's a Wonder Bundle, all right. What'll we do now?"

"Don't be too upset," said Minnie. "I think this really is a magic Wonder Bundle. We can use it to make a nice surprise for your Uncle Mickey. The only other thing we need is glue. And I just happen to have some."

Minnie got the glue and went to work with the rocks, the box, and the piece of cloth. Morty and Ferdie helped. "Now," she said. "Isn't that better? Your Uncle Mickey will have a nice paperweight and a pretty box to keep his paper clips in. I'll help you wrap them."

The next day, Morty and Ferdie gave Uncle Mickey his gifts. "These are wonderful birthday presents!" Mickey said. "They're just what I needed. Now I can keep my desk neat."

"Aunt Minnie was right," Morty said to Ferdie. "It was a marvelous, magic Wonder Bundle after all."

Desk-Top Presents

To make the paper-clip box, Minnie used a box with a slide-out drawer. She cut a piece of felt big enough to fit around the outside part. Then she spread glue all over the outside and glued the felt down. She covered the ends of the drawer with two small pieces of felt.

Minnie glued small rocks to the top of the box to make a pretty design— and glued a little rock to the drawer to make a knob.

To make the paperweight, Minnie glued three flat rocks together with the biggest one on the bottom. She glued a piece of felt to the bottom of the biggest rock, so that the paperweight wouldn't scratch Mickey's desk.

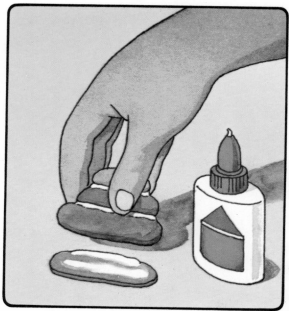

Picture This!

Minnie wanted to make a birthday present for Mickey, too—and, of course, she wanted it to be something very special. She thought about it for a long time. "Why, I know what Mickey thinks is special," she said suddenly. "It's having neat nephews like Morty and Ferdie—and a good friend like me—and a special dog like Pluto."

Minnie picked out her favorite pictures of Mickey, Morty, Ferdie, and herself—and one of Pluto, too. She used them to make Mickey a wall hanging full of favorite, friendly faces.

On the next page, you'll see how Minnie made Mickey's special birthday present. You can make one, too—for someone in your family or for a special friend.

What you'll need

Construction paper
Photos of people
Stick-on decorations

Yarn, ribbon,
  or felt
Glue

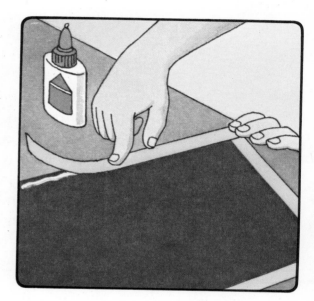

1. Glue two pieces of dark construction paper together to make a stiff picture board.

2. Cut four 1/2-inch (1.25 centimeter) strips from the long side of a different color of construction paper. Trim two of the strips to fit the short sides of the picture board. Glue the strips around the edges of the board to make a frame.

3. Choose the pictures you need. Cut them into different sizes and interesting shapes, and glue them to the picture board.

4. Frame each picture with something different—stick-on decorations, felt, ribbon, or yarn.

5. Finally, glue stars, flower stickers, or other decorations in several places on the dark background.

 Jiminy Cricket says, "Make sure it's okay to cut up the pictures you choose. And ask for help with cutting if you need it."

A Very Helpful Mending Kit

Morty had been at Daisy's house playing with Dewey. On his way home, he stopped at Minnie's house. "Do you know that a button is missing from your shirt?" Minnie asked him.

"Yes, I know," said Morty. "Daisy was going to sew one on for me, but she couldn't find a button the right size. But that didn't make any difference. She couldn't find a needle and thread, either."

"I'll sew your button on," said Minnie. "Then we'll make Daisy a very helpful mending kit. She can use it to keep all her mending things in one place."

Daisy was delighted when Minnie brought her the mending kit. "What a thoughtful gift," she said. "Now I have a place to keep needles and pins and scissors and thread."

"Oops!" said Minnie. "Now you have a place to use them, too. I'll be your first customer."

What you'll need

Egg carton   Rickrack
Material   Scissors
Cotton   Drinking straws
String   Needles, thread, pins,
Glue   and other mending things

Jiminy Cricket says,
"Ask for help with
cutting if you need it."

1. Cut a strip of material about 4 inches (10.2 centimeters) wide and 20 inches (51 cm) long. Glue rickrack over one of the long edges.

2. Close the carton and put glue along the outside edge of the top. Glue the other long edge of the material around the carton, pleating it as you glue it on.

3. Cut a piece of material about 1/2 inch (1.25 cm) smaller than the carton. Glue it onto the top, covering the edge of the skirt. Decorate it with rickrack.

4. Open the egg carton. Inside the top is a middle part that sticks up. Cut a slot through this part to hold scissors.

5. To make pincushions, stuff two 4-inch (10.2 cm) squares of material with cotton and tie them with string. Glue them into egg cups, with the tied part down.

6. Make little spools from 1-inch (2.5 cm) pieces of drinking straw. Wind them with different colors of thread. Cut a slit in each straw to hold the end of the thread.

7. Fill the pincushions and egg cups with needles, pins, thread, and other mending things.

Pocketful of Fun

When Morty and Ferdie arrived at Minnie's house, both of them were talking at the same time. "What's the matter?" asked Minnie. "I can't understand either of you when you both talk at the same time. Morty, you talk first and tell me what's bothering you."

"We just walked by Donald Duck's house, and we saw Huey, Louie, and Dewey sitting on the porch with their chins in their hands," Morty said. "They're going to Grandma Duck's farm, and they're afraid they'll have nothing to do."

"Nothing to do!" laughed Minnie. "If they are going to visit Grandma Duck, she'll find plenty of things to keep them busy."

"I guess you're right," said Ferdie. "But Huey and Dewey and Louie were saying that Grandma Duck doesn't have toys for them to play with. And Donald

said that there wouldn't be room in their luggage for big toys and games."

"I can take care of that," said Minnie. "I'll make some little games that they can put in their pockets and take with them."

Here are the pocket games Minnie made. You can make some to take on a trip—or give to a friend.

First Minnie made a jigsaw puzzle. She found a pretty picture of a robin. She glued the picture to a piece of construction paper the same size. When the glue dried, she cut the picture up to make a jigsaw puzzle. She put the puzzle in an envelope and wrote "Robin Puzzle" on it.

Next, Minnie made a letter game. First she drew lots of squares on a sheet of heavy paper. Next she printed a letter of the alphabet in each square. She made three sets of alphabet letters. Then she cut the squares apart along the lines.

Minnie put the letter squares into an envelope. On the front, she wrote "Letter Game." She wrote the directions, too: "Draw 12 letters. Make as many words as you can with the letters. Write down the words you make."

Finally, Minnie made a checker game. To make the checkerboard, she cut a 6-inch (15-centimeter) square from heavy paper. Then she made marks 3/4 inch (or 2 cm) apart on each side. She drew straight lines across and down to make checkerboard squares.

Next, starting with the lower, left-hand square, Minnie colored every other square black to make a checkerboard design. She folded the checkerboard in half and put it into an envelope.

Then Minnie got out her sewing basket. She picked out twelve dark buttons and twelve light buttons to use for checkers. She put the buttons in the envelope and wrote "Mini Checkers" on the front.

Shades for Sunny Days

One bright, hot day Minnie saw Daisy and Donald on their way to the beach with a big picnic basket. Daisy and Donald weren't wearing hats, and both of them were already squinting in the bright sunshine. Minnie thought to herself, "If the sun bothers their eyes that much, they won't have any fun at the beach."

"Donald, Daisy, wait a minute," Minnie called. "I have something for you."

Minnie ran inside her house. She brought out two large paper plates and a pair of scissors. With a few snips, she made two sun hats for Daisy and Donald to wear on their picnic.

"Why, thanks, Minnie," Daisy said. "This is just what we needed."

"Great idea!" Donald told her. "Sand and sun, here we come!"

Make some paper-plate sun hats for a party or picnic. You can wear them at the beach or in your own yard.

What you'll need

2 large paper plates   Pencil
Ruler   Scissors

Jiminy Cricket says, "Ask for help with cutting if you need it."

Daisy's Hat

1. On the back of the plate, draw a large + across the flat part. End the lines where the plate begins to curve. Then draw lines between the first lines to make an X.

2. Starting at the center, cut along each line. Stop where the line ends—don't cut the edge.

3. Turn the plate right side up. Pull the hat down gently over your head. Bend the front brim to shade your eyes.

Donald's Hat

1. Follow steps 1 and 2 above.

2. Cut away half of the inner sections of the paper plate.

3. Put the hat on in the same way, with the cut-away part in front. Pull the front down. Turn the back brim up.

Dandy Candy

Every time Goofy saw Minnie baking cakes and pies, he sighed. He knew that eating too many sweets isn't good for a person—but he also had a very big sweet tooth!

Minnie decided that a special little treat would be just the thing to make Goofy happy. So she made some of her famous haystack candy and put it in a pretty jar that she decorated herself.

When Goofy came to visit Minnie in the afternoon, she gave him the jar of candy. Of course, he had to

taste just one piece right away! "Garsh," he said. "This sure is dandy candy. It was awfully sweet of you to make it for me."

You can make Minnie's famous haystack candy, too.

What you'll need

Small pan	Wax paper
Bowl	Cookie sheet
Mixing spoon	1 cup chocolate chips
Fork	2 cups flaked coconut

1. Melt the chocolate chips over very low heat, stirring as they melt.

2. Put the coconut and melted chocolate in the bowl. Mix them thoroughly.

3. Cover the cookie sheet with wax paper. Pick up forkfuls of the candy mixture and put them on the wax paper. Press each candy haystack lightly with the back of the fork. Refrigerate the candy at least two hours. Then put it in a jar.

Minnie's candy jar is a large peanut butter jar. Minnie spreads glue on the lid and then covers it with material, leaving extra material around the edge. She wraps ribbon around the lid and ties a bow.

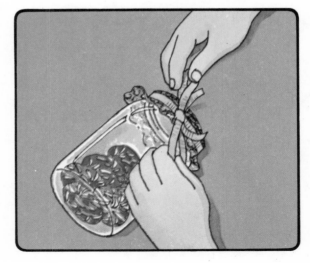

 Jiminy Cricket says, "Ask a grown-up to help you melt the chocolate chips."

Giggles for Minnie

What did Morty and Ferdie give Minnie for her birthday? Giggles! They made a book of their favorite birthday riddles to give her.

What did the angry birthday candle say?

"Having to be at all of these birthday parties really burns me up!"

What did the used-up birthday candle say to the new birthday candle?

"I've been feeling very rundown lately."

When is a birthday present like a prizefighter?

When it is boxed.

What is the best thing to put into a birthday cake?

Your teeth.

What is a baby whale after it is one year old?

Two years old.

What is long, green, and slippery and has "Happy Birthday" written on it?

A birthday snake.

If you open a gift when the sun shines on your birthday, what do you open when it rains on your birthday?

An umbrella.

Something Special for Minnie

Mickey wanted to give Minnie something special for her birthday. After all, she always made such wonderful presents to give to her friends. "What kind of present can I make for Minnie?" he wondered. "I know she likes plants—but plants are things you grow, not things you make."

Then Mickey got a wonderful idea. He could make Minnie a terrarium! It didn't take him long to find the perfect thing to use for a terrarium—a large, plastic soft-drink bottle. He found some very small plants to put in it.

"Oh, Mickey, what a clever idea," Minnie said. "It's just what I wanted!"

Mickey blushed. "Aw, it's nothing," he said. "Besides, it's about time *I* made a present for *you*."

You can make a terrarium for someone who likes plants. The little plants can be grouped to look like a tiny forest.

What you'll need

Large plastic soft drink bottle	Small stones
2 or 3 small plants	Sticks
Artificial flowers or bugs	Potting soil

1. Soak the bottle in very warm water for a few minutes. Then empty it, pull off the colored bottom part, and peel off the label.

2. Clean the glue out of the bottom part.

3. Put a layer of small rocks in the bottom part. Put some soil over the rocks, and then put in your plants. Be sure to press the roots down. Then add more soil around the plants to fill the planter. Arrange pretty stones, tiny sticks, or tiny toy animals around the plants.

4. Use a sharp knife to cut the top off the clear part of the bottle, about four inches from the cap. Turn the clear part upside down. Slip the cut edges into the planter to make a dome top. You can glue an artificial flower or bug to the dome for decoration.

Jiminy Cricket says, "Ask for help in removing the glue and cutting the plastic bottle."

A Practical Pencil-Keeper

Grandma Duck wanted to write down a recipe for Huey to take to Minnie Mouse—but she couldn't find a pencil. "Goodness gracious!" she said. "All of my pencils must be off on a pencil picnic. I can't keep a single one in the house!"

With a little help from Minnie, Huey made a gift that helped solve Grandma Duck's problem—a very practical pencil-keeper. (He also gave Grandma a few new pencils to keep.)

Grandma was very pleased with the present. "Why, thank you, Huey," she said. "I don't think I'll ever lose a pencil again. Oh, my goodness! Now, where did I put my keys?"

Look below to see how Huey made Grandma's pencil-keeper. Then make one for a special friend.

What you'll need

Empty spools (three or more)   Glue
Bright-colored ribbon or yarn   Plastic jar lid

1. Cut a piece of ribbon or yarn to wrap around the "wind-up" part of each spool. Make sure the piece is long enough to cover it completely.

2. Spread a little glue on the "wind-up" part of one spool. Wrap the spool with a piece of the ribbon or yarn. Make sure both ends are glued down tight.

3. Glue and wrap the rest of the spools in the same way. (You can mix or match the colors of ribbon or yarn.) Let the glue dry.

4. Arrange the spools inside the jar lid. Glue the bottom of each spool to the lid.

5. For decoration, glue an extra piece of yarn or a pretty ribbon around the outside of the lid.

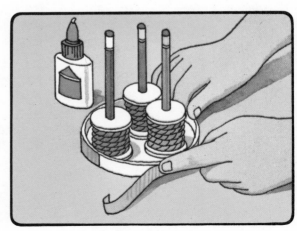

Mighty Flighty

One bright, windy day, Morty and Ferdie stopped by Minnie's house. "Why, hello, boys," she said. "Where are you going?"

"We've already been," Ferdie said. "We were flying our kite in the park—but the wind blew it into a tree. It's kind of wrecked."

"That's too bad," she said. She thought for a minute. "I don't have the things I need to make you another kite," she told them. "But I can make you some other things that fly."

In just a few minutes, Minnie made two things—a flying saucer and an airplane.

"Gee, that was fast!" Morty said.

"And easy," Ferdie added. "If the wind blows these into a tree, we can make more!"

Jiminy Cricket says, "Ask for help with cutting if you need it."

What you'll need

Paper plates	1 drinking straw
Glue	Tape
2 paper cups (without handles)	Scissors

Flying Saucer

Glue the paper plates together bottom to bottom. Wait a few minutes for the glue to dry. To fly your saucer, hold it flat and throw it with a flick of your wrist.

Ring-Wing Airplane

1. Measure 1 inch (2.5 centimeters) down from the top of each paper cup. Make a mark.

2. Starting at the mark, cut around each cup to make a ring.

3. Place one end of a drinking straw inside a ring. Tape the straw to the ring. Then tape the other end of the straw to the other ring. Make sure the wide ends of the paper-cup rings face the same way.

4. Lay the plane on a table with the straw down. Press down gently on each ring to make an oval shape. Your plane is ready to fly. Hold it with the wide ends of the rings forward when you throw.

FERDIE MORTY

It's A-maze-ing!

Morty and Ferdie ran outside to play with their flying saucer and ring-wing plane. But suddenly big, black clouds piled up in the sky, and cold, heavy raindrops began to spatter down.

When Morty and Ferdie came back inside, Minnie was ready for them. She was taping zigzag strips of cardboard into the lid of a shoe box.

"What's that?" Ferdie asked.

"Something for a rainy day," Minnie told him as she dropped a small ball into the lid. "Here—try it out. See if you can roll the ball through the maze from Start to Finish. Watch out for the traps—if you get caught, it's Morty's turn!"

You can make a maze puzzle like the one Minnie made.
It can be a rainy-day gift or a get-well present for a friend.

What you'll need

A shallow box lid	Scissors
Cardboard	Small rubber ball
Tape	Plastic wrap

1. Cut strips from the cardboard. Make them the same height as the sides of the box lid.

2. Use two strips for the first maze wall. Tape them down, leaving a "doorway" big enough for the ball to pass through.

3. Add more walls, leaving spaces for the ball to pass through in different places—at the far end, the near end, and the middle of the lid. Make sure you leave enough space between the walls for the ball to roll freely.

4. Make one or two traps in the maze. (Traps are dead-end paths that have no way out.) Mark one end of the maze "Start" and the other end "Finish."

5. Put the ball in the maze at "Start," and try out your maze puzzle. When it's working just right, tape plastic wrap over the top.

Jiminy Cricket says, "Ask for help with cutting if you need it."

A Piggy Bank
for Uncle Scrooge

"You know how much Uncle Scrooge likes to hoard his money," Louie said to Huey and Dewey. "Well, he has run out of places to put it!"

"I have an idea," said Dewey. "Let's make him a piggy bank where he can put his money."

Huey, Dewey, and Louie got all the things they would need from Minnie Mouse—and a few helpful hints, too. Minnie even gave them six pennies to put in the bank.

Uncle Scrooge liked his new piggy bank—and he was especially happy with the pennies he found in it.

You can make a piggy bank, too. The directions are on the next page. Put some pennies in it and give it to a friend who likes to save money.

What you'll need

A one-gallon plastic bleach
   bottle
Two large, dark buttons
Black rickrack or felt
Ribbon or material for a bow

4 twist-off soft-drink caps
White felt
Pink felt
Twist tie
Glue

Jiminy Cricket says,
"Ask for help with
cutting if you need it."

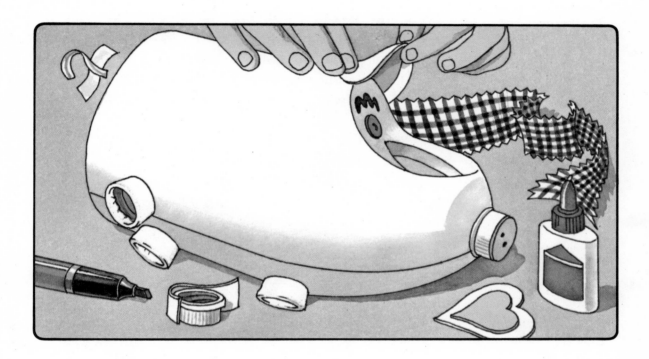

1. Wash and rinse the bottle thoroughly. Lay the bottle on its side with the handle up and cut a coin slot 3 inches (7.6 centimeters) below the handle.

2. Cut strips of felt a little wider than the bottle caps. Glue a felt strip around each cap, folding the extra felt over the edge. Glue the caps to the bottle for legs.

3. Cut two white felt hearts 3½ inches (9 cm) wide and two pink felt hearts 3 inches (7.6 cm) wide. Glue each pink heart inside a white heart. Fold back the rounded parts of each heart and glue the hearts to the bottle for ears.

4. Cut a piece of pink felt the same size as the bottle cap. Glue it to the cap. Put the cap on the bottle and draw two dots for a nose.

5. Curl the twist tie and glue it to the back of the piggy for a tail. Glue on buttons for eyes and felt or rickrack for eyebrows.

6. Wrap ribbon or material around the piggy behind the front legs and tie a big bow.

Twist It and Tie It

Morty and Ferdie were invited to a friend's birthday party—and their friend was a girl. They couldn't decide what kind of birthday present to get her.

"She doesn't play football," the boys told Minnie, "but she doesn't wear ruffles and stuff, either. She likes to roller skate and ride horseback."

"I have an idea for a gift you can make," said Minnie. "And I'll show you how to make it. You can make your friend a yarn belt to go with her jeans."

"Good idea," said Morty. "Let's get started!"

You can make a yarn belt, too. The directions are on the next page. Twisting and tying is easier if two people work together—so team up with a friend and make two belts!

34

What you'll need
Heavy yarn (2 colors)
4 pop-up squirters from liquid detergent bottles

1. Measure and cut three pieces, 6 feet (183 centimers) long, of each color of yarn. Put the pieces together and tie a knot about 6 inches (15.2 cm) from the end.

2. Take one color of yarn in each hand. Twist the colors around each other 3 times and then tie a double knot.

3. Have your friend hold the knot. Twist the colors 3 times again and tie another knot. Continue holding, twisting, and tying until about 6 inches (15.2 cm) of yarn are left. Then knot all the pieces together.

4. At both ends of the belt, twist each color of yarn tightly and slip the ends into the small hole of a pop-up squirter. Push the squirter up the yarn and tie a knot 2 inches (5.1 cm) from the end. Pull the squirter down to cover the knot.

 Jiminy Cricket says, "Ask for help with measuring if you need it."

Wrap It Up!

Minnie thinks that the package a present comes in should be just as nice as the present is. She goes out of her way to make her presents look special!

Minnie knows that Morty and Ferdie like to read the comics in the Sunday paper. So once she wrapped their presents in the Sunday comics. She tied bright-colored yarn around each box.

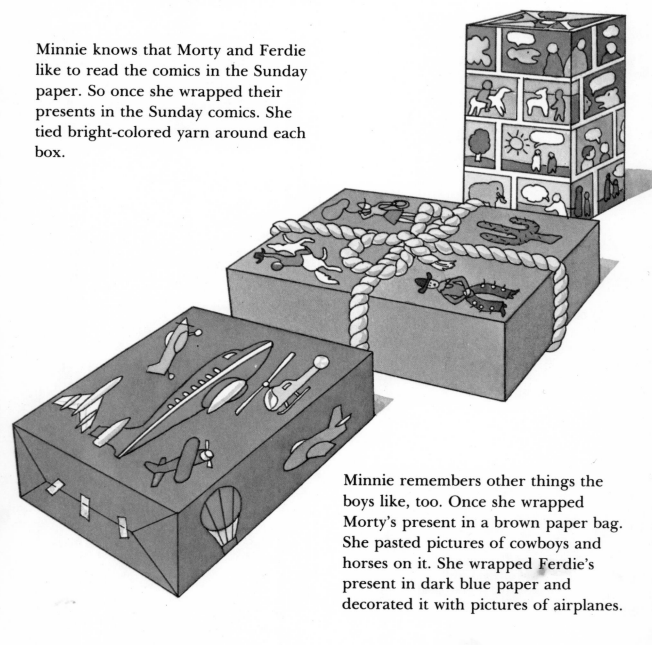

Minnie remembers other things the boys like, too. Once she wrapped Morty's present in a brown paper bag. She pasted pictures of cowboys and horses on it. She wrapped Ferdie's present in dark blue paper and decorated it with pictures of airplanes.

Minnie decided to make a well-dressed present for Mickey. First she wrapped the box in plain paper. Then she used a ruler to make two straight lines down the top of the box. She drew a pointed collar, too.

Minnie found some small white buttons in her sewing box. She glued them on the box between the lines.

Finally, Minnie cut a bright-colored strip from a plastic bread bag. She tied a bow to make a "real" bow tie, and glued the tie between the points of the collar.

Minnie made a very special package for Daisy's gift. The box was so nice that Daisy saved it to keep her jewelry in. Here is how to make one:

What you'll need

Oatmeal box	Scissors
Material	Glue
Felt	Cloth flowers

1. Cut a square of material 5 inches (12.7 centimeters) wider than the bottom of the box. Lay the square out right side down.

2. Take off the top. Cut the box down so that the sides are 2 inches (5.1 cm) tall. Cover all of the outside with glue.

3. Put the box in the center of the material.

4. Coat the inside of the box with glue. Pull the material up and into the box so that it sticks to the sides, both inside and out.

5. Cut a round piece of felt a little smaller than the bottom of the box. Glue it inside the box so that it covers the bottom.

6. Glue a large wad of cotton to the top of the box to make a cushion. Then cut another square of material and cover the box top the same way you did the box. Glue some pretty flowers to the top.

Jiminy Cricket says, "Ask for help with cutting if you need it."

Special Cards from Minnie

Minnie likes to make special cards and mail them to her special friends. And since she thinks all of her friends are special, she makes lots of cards!

Minnie usually begins with a sheet of white typing paper or construction paper. First she folds the sheet in half. Then she folds it again in the other direction.

Minnie saves magazine pictures and pretty wrapping paper to decorate her cards. She trims a picture or cuts wrapping paper to fit the card and glues it to the front.

39

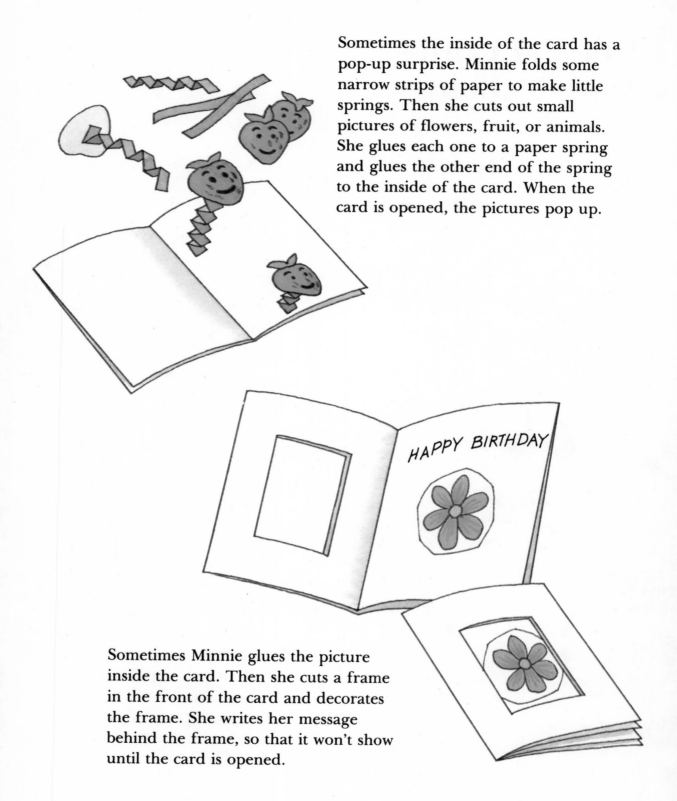

Sometimes the inside of the card has a pop-up surprise. Minnie folds some narrow strips of paper to make little springs. Then she cuts out small pictures of flowers, fruit, or animals. She glues each one to a paper spring and glues the other end of the spring to the inside of the card. When the card is opened, the pictures pop up.

HAPPY BIRTHDAY

Sometimes Minnie glues the picture inside the card. Then she cuts a frame in the front of the card and decorates the frame. She writes her message behind the frame, so that it won't show until the card is opened.

Minnie uses material to decorate her cards, too. This card looks like one of Grandma Duck's quilts! Minnie cut cloth flower petals from some checked material and used a different kind of material for the center of the flower.

Sometimes Minnie makes cards with cutout pictures. To make this card, she cut out a large picture of a butterfly. She folded a sheet of paper in half and glued the butterfly to the paper, with the top of its wings touching the fold. Then she cut all around the butterfly except for the top. This card opens from the bottom—and it's shaped just like a butterfly!

41

Messages from Minnie

Minnie tries to think up special messages for her cards. Of course, she wants each one to be just right for the person who gets the card—and she likes to think up a message that's just right for the card, too.

Here is a message she wrote to Mickey:

If you were a strawberry, I'd pick you to be my friend

Minnie

Here's a happy picture to brighten your day

Minnie

When Daisy was feeling sad, Minnie sent her a picture-frame card. She wrote:

I'm a sad sack

because I forgot your birthday!

Minnie

Sometimes Minnie's messages are jokes or rhymes. Minnie made a card from a paper bag. On it she wrote:

On a card with a picture of an owl, she wrote:

Take this wise old owl's advice and have a birthday that's extra nice.

I hope these flowers

will make you feel better!

Minnie

Minnie sent Goofy a get-well card decorated with flowers. She wrote: